Rain Forest at Night

RAIN FORESTS TODAY

Ted O'Hare

While hunting at night, a treefrog hugs a wide rain forest leaf.

Rourke
Publishing LLC
Vero Beach, Florida 32964

www.rourkepublishing.com

PHOTO CREDITS: All photos ©Lynn M. Stone except page 7 (main), 12, 13 ©James H. Carmichael

Editor: Frank Sloan

Cover and page design by Nicola Stratford

Library of Congress Cataloging-in-Publication Data

O'Hare, Ted, 1961-
  Rain forest at night / Ted O'Hare.
     p. cm. -- (Rain forests today)
  Includes bibliographical references (p.   ) and index.
    ISBN 1-59515-155-9 (hardcover)
  1. Rain forest animals--Juvenile literature. 2. Rain forest ecology--Juvenile literature. I. Title. II.
Series: O'Hare, Ted, 1961- Rain forests today.
  QL112.O39 2004
  591.734--dc22
                              2004006060

Printed in the USA

CG/CG

Table of Contents

Night and Darkness

Even during daylight, most of the tropical rain forest is dark. But night is inky black, like the inside of a dark cave.

A lot goes on in the forest at night. The daytime animals hide, but the **nocturnal** animals appear. They have ways to survive the dark of the rain forest.

The last rays of sun fall on a darkening rain forest.

Strange Noises

Tropical rain forests are usually quiet. Even the falling rain is quiet.

All kinds of insects, including mosquitoes, buzz at night.

At night the silence is broken by howling monkeys and hooting owls. Frogs and toads call for mates. They croak and chirp.

The howler monkey roars at night in the rain forests of Mexico and Central and South America.

6

A mantid insect hunts from its leafy perch.

A three-toed sloth hangs on a branch as night falls in the rain forest.

Mammals

Many four-footed animals are active at night. Big cats prowl silently as they listen and sniff for **prey**. The biggest cats are the jaguars of South America and the rare tigers of Southeast Asia.

A **sloth** munches leaves, and the big-eyed **loris** eats insects, lizards, fruit, and plants in the **canopy**.

A rare Sumatran tiger wades through a rain forest stream at dusk.

Snakes

Many rain forest snakes hunt best at night. Pit vipers are a group of poisonous snakes. They include the **fer de lance** and other species. A pit viper doesn't need to see or hear its prey. It has an organ that senses heat. It can find a mouse from the mouse's body heat.

A Wagler's palm viper hunts in the darkness of a rain forest in Malaysia.

The colorful eyelash viper of Central and South America has spiny "eyelash" scales above its eyes.

Bats

Bats are flying mammals. Many kinds of bats live in tropical rain forests. By day they hang from trees. At night most of the bats fly around.

They catch insects by sending out high-pitched squeaks. The bat's squeak strikes an object. Then the squeak echoes, or bounces, back to the bat. The echo tells the bat where to find its prey.

Bats roost at dawn on a log over a rain forest stream.

Frogs and Toads

Most frogs and toads go about at night. Females locate males by hearing their calls. Frogs and toads lay their eggs at night.

Many frogs have large eyes. Their night vision is probably very good, but their sense of touch is better. Many frogs catch insects when the insects touch them!

A red-eyed treefrog waits for nocturnal insects.

Spiders

Spiders are **arachnids**, or eight-legged creatures. They are active in the rain forest at night. Scorpions, tarantulas, and wolf spiders all hunt at night.

The "furry" tarantula has eight eyes as well as eight legs. The eyes may help the spider find its prey, mostly insects, in dim light.

The Indian ornamental tarantula is a large "hairy" spider of Asia.

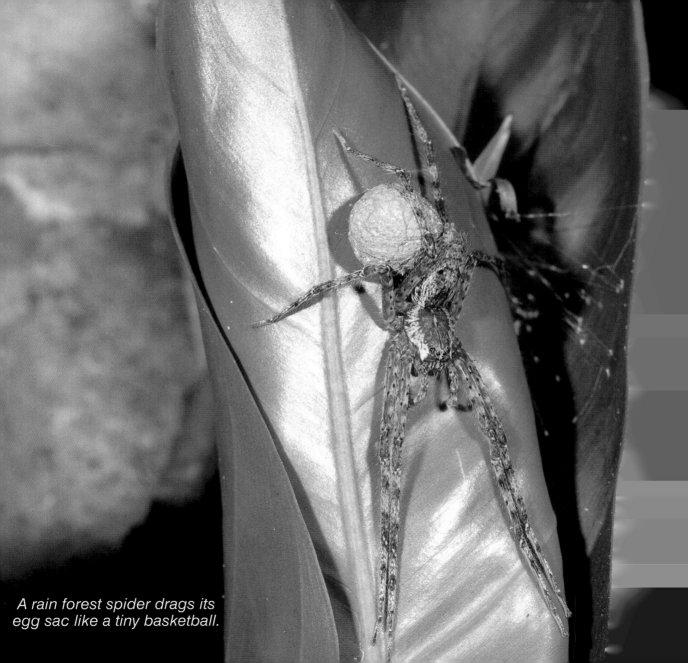

A rain forest spider drags its egg sac like a tiny basketball.

Leaf-cutting Ants

The amazing leaf-cutting ant carries pieces of leaves to its burrow. The ant chews the leaves and then spits them out. The ant adds a liquid to the leaf matter.

A **fungus** soon appears on the leaf matter. The fungus then becomes food for the ants.

Leaf-cutter ants carry leaf pieces down a tree trunk.

Moths

Most moths fly at night. Moths fly quietly, on soft wings. Because they are so quiet when they fly, moths can hear very well. Some hear so well they can even escape from bats. Some moths also have a sharp sense of smell. A male moth can find a female from her scent.

Unlike moths, butterflies fly during the day.

A saturnid moth with "see-through" wing spots rests on a limb.